ARLINGTON

[a love story]

T0165844

BOOKS BY ENDA WALSH
PUBLISHED BY TCG

Ballyturk

The New Electric Ballroom and *The Walworth Farce*

Lazarus
A Musical by David Bowie and Enda Walsh

Once
Book by Enda Walsh
Music and Lyrics by Glen Hansard and Markéta Irglová

Penelope

The Small Things and Other Plays

ALSO INCLUDES:

The Ginger Ale Boy
Disco Pigs
misterman
bedbound
How These Desperate Men Talk
Lynndie's Gotta Gun
Chatroom

ARLINGTON

[a love story]

Also includes
ROOMS

Enda Walsh

THEATRE COMMUNICATIONS GROUP
NEW YORK
2017

Arlington [a love story] is published by Theatre Communications Group, Inc., 520 Eighth Avenue, 24th Floor, New York, NY 10018-4156

This volume is published in arrangement with Nick Hern Books Limited, The Glasshouse, 49a Goldhawk Road, London, W12 8QP

This publication is made possible in part by the New York State Council on the Arts with the support of Governor Andrew Cuomo and the New York*State Legislature.

TCG books are exclusively distributed to the book trade by Consortium Book Sales and Distribution.

A catalogue record for this book is available from the Library of Congress.

ISBN 978-1-55936-550-5 (paperback)

Cover design by Lisa Govan
Cover photo of Charlie Murphy by Colm Hogan;
graphic image by Gareth Jones

First TCG Edition, May 2017

For Jo

CONTENTS

ARLINGTON

[a love story]

The world premiere of *Arlington [a love story]* took place at Leisureland, Salthill, Galway on July 11, 2016, as part of the 2016 Galway International Arts Festival. It was produced by Landmark Productions and Galway International Arts Festival. The cast was as follows:

Isla	Charlie Murphy
Young Man	Hugh O'Conor
Young Woman	Oona Doherty
Voices	Eanna Breathnach, Olwen Fouéré, Helen Norton, Stephen Rea
Director	Enda Walsh
Choreographer	Emma Martin
Composer	Teho Teardo
Designer	Jamie Vartan
Lighting Designer	Adam Silverman
Sound Designer	Helen Atkinson
Video Designer	Jack Phelan

Characters

ISLA
YOUNG MAN
YOUNG WOMAN

VOICES

MICHAEL
MAUREEN
THE USUAL MAN
SUPERVISOR

This text went to press before the end of rehearsals and so may differ slightly from the play as performed.

Scene One

A curtain opens from the middle.

A realistic waiting room – of no fixed time or place.

Its paint and walls blistering – worn carpet tiles, square foam ceiling tiles.

A large rectangle window on the stage-left wall (the bottom sill, five foot off the floor). A curtain/blind that covered the window has fallen on the floor. There is no glass – it is open to the outside.

Beneath the window is a 1950s radio sitting on a thin-legged wooden table.

Against the stage-right wall is a row of three blue plastic chairs joined together and pinned to the floor.

A large Swiss cheese plant stands upstage of these chairs.

Above the chairs is a large map of an undefined city.

There are small overhead security cameras in each corner.

Very downstage on the stage-right wall is a wall-mounted thin intercom microphone.

Very downstage on the stage-left wall is a wall-mounted orange ticket-dispenser.

There's nothing on the large back wall – but for an old radiator.

High in the upstage-left corner is a long LED number display screen with the number '3097' showing.

Mirroring this – in the upstage-right corner – is a large square industrial gas heater.

Beneath this heater – piled in the corner – are clothes, shoes, personal artefacts…

Standing centre-stage looking up at the window is a young woman in a sweatshirt, skirt, socks and runners.

This is ISLA ['Aye-la'].

The sounds of some seagulls can be heard through the open window.

We watch her for some moments.

The radio suddenly switches itself on.

A radio drama's theme music is heard.

A daily radio play begins – sounds from a farmhouse kitchen where a radio is playing in the background.

MICHAEL. Good morning, Maureen!

MAUREEN. Oh my God, is it, though? You'd have to wonder whether it is. The rain, my God!

MICHAEL. It'll be good for the fields. We need it we do.

MAUREEN. Oh we do, Michael. The summer was bone dry – you'd forget it in the autumn what with the rain of lately.

MICHAEL. Sure that's it – people forget stuff.

MAUREEN. We are forgetful, that's right.

ISLA *sits on the floor and begins to take off her runners and socks.*

MICHAEL. And how's Fidelma?

MAUREEN. Oh Fidelma's fine.

MICHAEL. Is she?

MAUREEN. She is yeah.

MICHAEL. Look, that's not what I heard. As a friend I think that it's only fair that I raise this worry with you, Maureen.

The lights above ISLA *fade up slowly. It's a power surge.*

MAUREEN. A worry? Is it a worry, Michael?

MICHAEL. Well yes it is.

MAUREEN. Or is it just malicious gossip!

MICHAEL. Look – the word is… Fidelma is acting a little strange…

MAUREEN. Enough of this rubbish! Fidelma is my daughter, Michael! My daughter! Yes in the past she has been wayward! We all know that! No one will ever forgive her the time she kicked that dog in Donavan's!

ISLA stands and looks up at the lights, never having experienced this before. The sound of the radio play begins to rise in volume erratically.

MICHAEL. He ate her toasted sandwich of course!

MAUREEN. Exactly, Michael! With Fidelma there's always a good reason for kicking a dog!

MICHAEL. But how can you explain what she did to Bernice Boyle?!

MAUREEN. An accident of the universe, that's all!

MICHAEL. She ran over Bernice's foot in her Toyota…!

The lights too bright – they blow with a noise.

Blackout and silence.

In the darkness we hear someone stumble over –

A head smashes against a lamp –

ISLA. Hello?

A glass falls on the ground. A tray of glasses falls on the ground.

A cacophony of various large things hitting the ground is heard.

It eventually stops.

The YOUNG MAN's *pained heavy breath is heard amplified in the auditorium.*

Then –

YOUNG MAN. Hello?

ISLA. Something's happened with the power.

YOUNG MAN. Is this, emm… Is this a microphone?

Sound of a microphone being hit repeatedly –

Yeah. (*Slight pause.*) Are you hearing me? Is… Isla? – your name.

The lights surge back on – the radio switches back on but barely audible now.

ISLA *is facing the stage-right wall.*

ISLA. What happened?

YOUNG MAN. The, em – I've no idea – Something.

ISLA. Will it happen again?

YOUNG MAN. I hope not.

ISLA. Where's the usual man?

YOUNG MAN. What d'ya mean?

ISLA. The one who usually sits where you're sitting.

YOUNG MAN. Oh he's, em…

ISLA. He's not gone, has he?

YOUNG MAN. I suppose he has, yeah – he's sorta gone.

ISLA. But where to?

YOUNG MAN. I don't know for sure.

ISLA. Has he gone on holidays?

YOUNG MAN. It's a bit more permanent than that.

ISLA. You mean he's left?

YOUNG MAN. That's right, yeah.

ISLA. He didn't say anything about leaving.

YOUNG MAN. No he didn't.

ISLA. I mean to me – he never said he was leaving to me.

YOUNG MAN. Oh right. Well he wouldn't.

ISLA. Wouldn't he?

YOUNG MAN. Wouldn't he?

ISLA. Well it's a little unusual.

YOUNG MAN. Oh is it?

ISLA. For him, yeah.

YOUNG MAN. Well people do change – it does happen.

ISLA. I don't believe that.

YOUNG MAN. Don't you?

ISLA. That he'd wake up one morning and decide not to come to work – I don't think that's him at all.

YOUNG MAN. Well maybe…

ISLA. I thought we had got close – well as close as you can get with a person like him.

YOUNG MAN. You must have talked a lot…

On the other side of the downstage-right wall, where the microphone is – a light fades up on the YOUNG MAN *sitting at a large desk and looking at various monitors showing* ISLA. *He speaks through a microphone.*

ISLA. Yeah there was a lot of talk. Some music and entertainment-of-a-sort but mostly just talking, you know. My plans and dreams and stuff.

YOUNG MAN. And he was a good listener?

ISLA. Mostly, yeah. It's not the easiest of jobs.

YOUNG MAN. There are worse jobs.

ISLA. Really? What sort?

YOUNG MAN. Well I imagine there are – is what I mean.

ISLA. Right. He's really left?

YOUNG MAN. Yeah it's just me now.

ISLA. From now on?

YOUNG MAN. Yeah I suppose so.

ISLA. We haven't spoken before, me and you?

YOUNG MAN. No never. First time.

ISLA. Actually you sound much younger than him.

YOUNG MAN. Than who?

ISLA. The usual man – the man before.

YOUNG MAN. Well I am actually. I'm a lot younger than him.

ISLA. Not colleagues then – you and him?

YOUNG MAN. Not now no.

ISLA. How old are you exactly?

YOUNG MAN. Am I allowed to get personal?

ISLA. Don't you know the rules?

YOUNG MAN. Of course I know the rules! I'm here, amn't I?!

ISLA. Actually he never really got that personal. He talked a lot
   about himself but it's impossible to say whether he was
   really his words, if you know what I mean. Maybe don't get
   too personal.

YOUNG MAN. Just to be on the safe side.

ISLA. I don't want to get you into trouble.

YOUNG MAN. Can you do that?

ISLA. I'll try not to.

YOUNG MAN. Thank you.

ISLA. You sound very nervous by the way.

YOUNG MAN. Right well…

ISLA. I can hear it in your voice.

YOUNG MAN. Oh.

ISLA. What do you look like?

YOUNG MAN. Like my mother.

ISLA. And what's that?

YOUNG MAN. Rangy and pale.

ISLA. Are you handsome?

A slight pause.

YOUNG MAN. Not really, no.

ISLA. You're not just saying that?

YOUNG MAN. Well in a certain light I can be – in a very dark-ish light.

ISLA. Oh. Do you think I'm attractive?

YOUNG MAN. Honestly?

ISLA. You can lie if you like, I don't mind.

YOUNG MAN. I won't lie – I'm a terrible liar.

ISLA. Well do you think I'm attractive?

YOUNG MAN. Sort of.

ISLA. I think that's a bit too honest.

YOUNG MAN. Sort-of attractive is better than a bit attractive.

ISLA. Really?

YOUNG MAN. It's also a little better than slightly attractive.

ISLA. What parts of me are sort-of attractive?

YOUNG MAN. You've got a nice head.

ISLA. Oh.

YOUNG MAN. And shoulders.

ISLA. Head and shoulders.

YOUNG MAN. That's your top two.

ISLA. And what parts of me are only slightly attractive…?

YOUNG MAN. Your feet.

ISLA. Right.

YOUNG MAN. But then I hate feet. As a child I used get sick
when I looked at feet.

ISLA. Really?

YOUNG MAN. I dreaded the summer –

ISLA. Oh.

YOUNG MAN. Because of the sandals. I'd puke everywhere. It
was exhausting! My mother used blindfold me before she
put on my socks. I'm a lot better now.

ISLA. Would you prefer if I was wearing socks and runners?

YOUNG MAN. Absolutely yeah.

*She sits on the floor and starts putting on her socks and
runners –*

ISLA. You're quite interesting.

YOUNG MAN. Am I?

ISLA. I think it's the longest conversation I've ever had.

YOUNG MAN. That's not a bad thing, is it?

ISLA. Well not for me, no.

YOUNG MAN. I love to talk.

ISLA. Right.

YOUNG MAN. I don't get to do it much myself – but when I
do – I really enjoy talking. Thirty-two, by the way.

ISLA. What?

YOUNG MAN. My age. Thirty-two years.

ISLA. I used to want to know my age but as the years go by I
think about it less and less. How old do I look to you?

YOUNG MAN. About thirty-two.

ISLA. With or without socks?

YOUNG MAN. There's not much in it.

ISLA. It's sort of a non-age age.

YOUNG MAN. Right.

ISLA. Neither young or old?

YOUNG MAN. Yeah it's a middling-sort-a-number.

ISLA. Mediocre, really.

YOUNG MAN. It doesn't have the gravitas of thirty-three.

ISLA. No you're right.

She holds out her 'runnered' feet.

YOUNG MAN. Thank you for that.

ISLA. It's fine.

YOUNG MAN. How come you weren't sleeping earlier?

A slight pause.

What?

ISLA. Were you watching me not sleeping?

YOUNG MAN. I don't think that's wrong, is it?

ISLA. It might be wrong.

YOUNG MAN. When I arrived and sat down I could see on the monitors that you were upset about something.

ISLA. Yeah I was.

YOUNG MAN. About what?

ISLA. You didn't make my curtain fall from the window, did you?

YOUNG MAN. When did it fall?

ISLA. Early last night.

YOUNG MAN. Right.

ISLA. I spoke to the usual man about it but he never responded.

YOUNG MAN. And the curtain falling kept you from sleeping?

ISLA. No – what I saw outside the window kept me from sleeping.

A sign above the YOUNG MAN*'s head saying 'SEND' buzzes on.*

YOUNG MAN. Do you have anything you want – anything to tell me…?

ISLA. Is the conversation over?

YOUNG MAN. Only this part.

ISLA. Don't you want to hear about what I saw outside…?

YOUNG MAN. Not now no.

ISLA. Why not?

YOUNG MAN. I think we should make a start.

ISLA. You're sounding a little anxious…

YOUNG MAN (*anxiously*). I'm not anxious!

ISLA. I think you are.

YOUNG MAN. I think you're wrong actually!

ISLA. What have you got to be anxious about?

YOUNG MAN. Absolutely nothing!

ISLA. Then why do you sound anxious?

YOUNG MAN. I'm not hardly anxious a bit – not even slightly anxious!

ISLA. Your voice is going up.

YOUNG MAN (*laughing anxiously*). No it isn't!

ISLA. Yes it is.

YOUNG MAN. It is not!!

ISLA. A couple of octaves!

YOUNG MAN. What?!

ISLA. It's quite high!

YOUNG MAN. That's not true!

ISLA. Are you even sure that you're a man!?

YOUNG MAN. Look! – I need to report something! That's the job, isn't it!?

ISLA. Don't you know?

YOUNG MAN. Well of course I know!

ISLA. You don't really sound like you know very much – no wonder you're anxious.

YOUNG MAN. I don't want the Supervisor coming over to check on me, is what I mean!

ISLA. Right.

YOUNG MAN. It's best if I can send her something – so if you have anything you want to say…

ISLA (*dismissing him*). Yeah-yeah-yeah…

YOUNG MAN. Do you want me to help you with anything – is what I'm asking?

ISLA. Yes-of-course-I-want-your-help – that's your job!

YOUNG MAN. Exactly! Good.

ISLA. Good. (*Slight pause.*) Are you ready?

YOUNG MAN. No just let me, emmmmmmmmmm…

He clears the desk of THE USUAL MAN*'s sandwiches, crisps and drink with one sweep of his arm. It all crashes to the floor.*

Right.

He looks a little terrified at the various sound and visual equipment in front of him.

He touches one button and it gives him an electric shock.

(Jumping back.) Ahh!

A slight pause.

He tentatively steps back into the desk –

(Quietly to the desk.) You littttttlllllle shit…

Suddenly one of the machines noisily goes on fire.

Oh Jesus Christ!!

He crashes about the small room looking for a fire extinguisher.

ISLA. Is everything okay?

YOUNG MAN *(under pressure)*. Yes-yes – it's all fine! Just-gimme…

He finds the fire extinguisher – turns quickly and begins to extinguish the fire.

ISLA. What's going on?

YOUNG MAN. Nothing. *(Slight pause.)* Much.

The fire goes out.

He throws the extinguisher away – and sits down and settles himself into the work.

A pause.

(Calmly.) Isla?

ISLA. Yes.

YOUNG MAN. I'm ready now.

A slight pause.

Do you want some musical accompaniment, by the way?

ISLA. Yeah why not.

He lifts up a tiny synthesiser and puts it on the desk.

He brings down the fader on an old lighting desk – and the light in ISLA's room darkens – a single light on her now.

YOUNG MAN. All right then. I'm recording – in three…
two… one.

A pause.

ISLA (*to herself. Fed up*). Ohh Christ…

ISLA *starts something and speaks into the microphone on
the stage-right wall – her voice amplified.*

I thought that maybe I might set this one in, eh…
Summertime… If, emm… if I can get rid of that picture of
you puking on to your bare feet…

YOUNG MAN. Sorry.

ISLA. Let me just imagine that the weather's warm – the season
isn't that important, really – warm but not sandal weather
just yet… It's a sensory-piece anyway so…

She clears her throat.

She begins, somewhat disconnected at the start –

I'm in the countryside and I'm – I'm leaving an open field
behind me – walking away from that field. And maybe the
sun is on my back – that would be nice… And I'm…

The YOUNG MAN *starts to play something on the synthesiser
– but it immediately plays a terrible noise. He stops.*

YOUNG MAN. Sorry just…

*He tries something else – a loud samba rhythm begins to
play.*

Fuck it – sorry…

It stops.

After a little while he eventually finds an appropriate sound.

Okay carry on.

A pause.

ISLA. In the field – sun on my back… And I'm – I'm wearing a
shirt –

He plays simple long notes, accompanying her story –

– and let's say it's a, eh – a man's shirt I'm wearing – there's no good reason why it's a man's shirt – comfort, I suppose. I'm feeling comfortable in it. And I leave the open field and walk towards… what? (*Slight pause.*) These woods. Right. (*Slight pause.*) It's probably important to point out that these woods are wolf-free – there's nothing of that sort of menace about – the sort that's written in picture books – there are only animals there of the – very fluffy kind. Lambs and, eh – hamsters. And there are birds, definitely – not the gulls I can hear outside – but smaller sweeter birds – that walk me further into these woods.

A different more beautiful music mixes over what the YOUNG MAN *plays.*

And being careful underfoot then – and little twigs – and lovely uneven ground – and fingers passing over trees as I walk onwards. And through pools of sunlight bent through branches – and sat down then and warming my face – and catching again childhood this sun – and gently fall the leaves about me. I turn forward and towards – promise. (*Slight pause.*) Today my spirit will walk a distance. (*Slight pause.*) The moment will continue. (*Slight pause.*) The day will lead me. (*Slight pause.*) It will last, this feeling.

ISLA *turns away from the microphone – and faded up on the back wall are blurred images of a walk through those woods she imagined (though she's not visible).*

The music continues.

After thirty seconds the YOUNG MAN *cuts the images and music.*

The YOUNG MAN *speaks into his microphone.*

YOUNG MAN. How was that?

ISLA. Yeah fine. (*Slight pause.*) Actually it was nice.

YOUNG MAN. I'm glad.

A pause.

ISLA. Thank you… whoever you are.

YOUNG MAN. You're very welcome, Isla.

A slight pause.

Suddenly The Ramone's version of 'Baby, I Love You' blasts.

The YOUNG MAN *sits back in his seat. The light comes down on him and he is lost in a semi-darkness.*

ISLA *stands centre-stage facing the back.*

She turns her head to the right and looks up at the window.

Automatically, she then turns around and walks to the pile of clothes in the upstage-left corner.

She's made a head, arms, torso of a person out of clothes and bits and pieces.

She prepares it and places it sitting on the plastic seats.

She walks away from it – reaches the stage-left wall and turns sharply.

She mouths the lyrics of the song, and sings some out loud as she plays out a (rather elaborate) imagined seduction scene with this person as her companion.

The figure has seen better days – eyes and arms are hanging off it. At one point an arm flings across the room.

During this she gives up on her playing and drops the figure on the floor.

The back wall fills with video footage of a 1970's talk-show host talking to camera. It's stuck in a ten-second loop.

She looks back at him.

The lights and music surge around her.

ISLA. Oh fuck.

They cut momentarily into darkness and silence.

Lights up with the song continuing and video loop of the talk-show host reforming on the wall.

ISLA *walks over to the three plastic seats.*

She picks up a green ticket beside her.

'Baby, I Love You' ends.

The sound of the radio distant – barely audible.

ISLA *sits there for twenty seconds – waiting.*

She looks back at the talk-show host.

She then begins to talk to herself –

Of what I remember – and I might be wrong about this and probably am wrong – is that it was a little longer. I've this idea that it was little longer – that there was more to this telly-man – more than this ten-second reiteration – this talking words that I can't hear and him gesturing to someone that never comes. I mean, there must have been someone before – or afterwards even – for you'd imagine that someone might have arrived and joined this man on his comfortable-looking seats – and they might have sat down and talked about – whatever it is that people talk about. Ourselves obviously – we'll always have ourselves to talk about. So they would sit – let me imagine it – and they would have a conversation about…

She leaves her ticket down on the seat and walks over to the back wall 'to join' the talk-show host –

– I'm strugglin' to imagine what stories they might share with one another. People – let's say – have pasts, generally – and they could talk about all-a-that – and they would hypothetically get some – enjoyment might be too strong a word… (*And talking too fast.*) Right at this moment I can't reconcile why people would sit around on comfy seats and talk about what has already happened – but perhaps they did because they really needed to talk about it – or they were told to talk about it – or maybe they started talking about what could possibly happen – what a day could build into – the hope of that day – talking out their dreams in the way that people like me are told to talk them out – these lies.

She suddenly slaps her face.

A slight pause.

(*To herself.*) Don't.

A slight pause.

Of course they might just be sitting there and talking about cheese.

The image of the talk-show host disappears with noise from the wall.

A packet of Rich Tea biscuits rolls towards her. We see a small flap close on the stage-left wall.

She walks over and picks up the biscuits.

Thank you.

A cup of tea appears on the floor out of the stage-left wall.

She opens the biscuits and takes one – walks over and picks up the tea.

Thank you.

During the below the YOUNG MAN *is faded up behind the wall at his desk eating a sandwich – listening to her and looking at the monitor.*

ISLA *looks again at the figure she danced with as it lies on the floor beneath her.*

When have I ever not wanted a companion to talk with? Never.

She lifts it up by the top of the head.

I've always wanted someone else – and if not always to talk to – to at least share this room and wait for my number to be called – to sit silently even and share the same air with another body beside mine would be nice.

The body snaps from the head and drops on the floor.

Suddenly the LED screen makes a noise and the numbers begin to flick. They stop on '4231'.

She plays a sad game with herself where she looks at each of the the numbers on her ticket and checks it with the number on the screen.

She gives the game up on the third number.

She walks back to the three plastic seats and places the ticket on the seat beside her.

With her finger she writes four large letters into the air. G–R–I–T.

She clenches her fist a little.

Then –

Yesterday evening and immediately after my trip away from that window when I was struck down with… impossible to put a word on what it was when I saw what I saw outside – but at that moment – the walking-away-from-the-window moment – my back to it – I said – Never again must you feel this grief – I may have clenched my fist and waved it at an imaginary me – like a parent berating a small child. I did feel like a lonely child just then and since – a little weakened by the waiting naturally and needing the – let me begin with the word steel and work a little backwards… the facility to keep on going. To implode is never an option in here – imploding lives in the same dream world as friendship – he told me that once when he was angry. I needed a stronger spirit so I could push through today with what I had seen outside and what I had realised when I returned to this chair and sat back down in the hope of sleep – to continue this waiting. Today I would need a new – grit. (*Slight pause.*) A very good word, grit. (*Spells it in the air with her finger again.*) G–R–I–T.

YOUNG MAN (*to himself*). Grit.

Through a straw the YOUNG MAN *noisily sucks up the end of a can of Club Orange.*

She briefly looks towards the wall like she's heard him through it.

The YOUNG MAN *leans in and stares at the monitor.*

She turns and crosses the space and stands beneath the window.

Then –

ISLA. To think new of myself is to walk back through different rooms where images are made not true. To lie and see me in a different world. And they shrink the room and harden the plastic seats – and no good and only to torture me, these lies – and even more now with this truth written big – but still to be in those crowds. To imagine the people. To be there walking with them. One last time maybe.

ISLA *covers her eyes.*

During the below two things happen.

A light comes down on her beneath the window and on the YOUNG MAN *in his space.*

And the back wall begins to fill with old images of a city and people she never knew – as a music fades up accompanying them.

It is all strangely – romantic.

And to walk myself through a version of the city that once was. (*Slight pause.*) My house is left and walked away from it – the terrace in which the house stands, it folds into the horizon and a train takes me with other people to the city. And there is purpose to my walking and definition to my day – a day that starts with a morning time and with minutes – it strolls forward. And we – 'cause I'm imagining me with another person – 'cause let's say I make myself a friend in this city – we are discussing our lives in terms of things that need doing by us. We're filed into offices – and in these places of work we're pursuing – goals we'll call them. And there's discussion and desks and chairs behind these desks, obviously – and ideas are taken from the air and made whole these ideas – and biscuits are eaten – a variety, let's say – and upon this food satisfaction will fall – with even more work accomplished after our lunches. And when the day is done – there's journeys back home in the evening – or maybe not home for me – but journeys elsewhere where there's noise and more food – where we meet and – him – 'cause it is a him this new friend – him and me meet and stretch out an evening with our talk of – you mustn't ever talk of love, Isla. And that day spins in this way – without noise it spins about inside and built on lies so it turns my insides sour – but still to see from above the city as how they were – as how people once lived – a place where love could be…

She lowers her hand – her eyes full of tears. The images and music continue –

YOUNG MAN. What are you doing…?

ISLA. I'm allowed to talk even when you haven't asked me to talk!

YOUNG MAN. I know that!

ISLA. I know you know that.

YOUNG MAN. But how are you doing that to the wall without me? The pictures…!

ISLA. You mean you're not doing this!?

YOUNG MAN. I thought it was all operated from…!

The YOUNG MAN *hammers at the equipment on the desk and the images and music cut – and suddenly a new voice is heard.*

It's the recorded voice of THE USUAL MAN *berating* ISLA –

THE USUAL MAN….and to feel the importance of you – to acknowledge and cherish the uniqueness of you – like you were plucked from the universe…

The YOUNG MAN *hits another button –*

…that singular heartbeat of yours – to touch your hand and draw that line from first breath to death…

The YOUNG MAN *hits another button. The lights are surging again during the below –*

...To be chosen and grown and cared and fed and envied – to be at the centre and honoured and blessed to be kept in this place. To be the sun and built about you this other universe – a world outside being made from your dreams, Isla – a city of people building your hopes – and to be called then and to walk out into those dreams – and to reunite with a family whose lives too are rebuilt – to be inside here and cared and allowed to dream a life – to be that family, to be that four-year-old, that deity, to be chosen and grown and cared and fed and envied – to be at the centre and honoured and blessed.

The sound cuts.

A long pause. Then –

YOUNG MAN. Was that him – the usual man?

ISLA. Yes.

YOUNG MAN. And that's how he usually talked?

ISLA. Lately. What's happening with the lights, do you think?

A slight pause.

YOUNG MAN. I don't know. (*Slight pause.*) Maybe it's all falling apart finally.

ISLA. It's me who's broken.

ISLA *walks and stands in the far downstage next to the stage-right wall – the* YOUNG MAN *directly in front of her – separated by the ten centimetres of wall.*

YOUNG MAN. Will you tell me what you remember?

ISLA. About what?

YOUNG MAN. How you came here.

ISLA. Why?

YOUNG MAN. Just to hear it.

ISLA. It's recorded – you can read it whenever you want.

YOUNG MAN. But just to hear it from you, I mean.

A pause.

ISLA. Do you know where he's gone – the man who used sit at the desk? (*Slight pause*.) Do you think he's going to come and take me from here like he always promised?

A long pause. The YOUNG MAN *can't answer her.*

Even if you're not that handsome – I like your voice by the way – I should have said that at the very start.

A pause.

YOUNG MAN. I like yours too. (*Slight pause*.) After your head and shoulders, it's probably my next favourite thing.

A pause.

ISLA. I think it's possible that if you stay from this moment on – I'll probably be fairly happy.

YOUNG MAN. Oh.

A pause.

ISLA. I meant really happy but I said fairly happy because I didn't want to sound too needy.

YOUNG MAN. I understand.

A pause.

ISLA. If I tell you what I remember about coming here will you tell me what's happening now?

A pause.

YOUNG MAN. Yes. (*Slight pause*.) Mostly.

A pause.

ISLA. Do you want me to start?

YOUNG MAN. Will you need any musical accompaniment?

ISLA. No – not that you weren't good before.

YOUNG MAN. It's fine…

ISLA. I've hurt your feelings.

YOUNG MAN. You haven't.

ISLA. Okay.

A slight pause.

YOUNG MAN. Go on.

A long pause.

Then –

ISLA. I'm four years old and our house is gone and we're
    walked towards these towers being built. And up these stairs
    inside this tower – and put into this room. And nights pass
    and the door opens and they take my dad and sister. (*Slight
    pause.*) A brother next to leave. And more tears probably.
    And food delivered as always – and the memory of my four
    years out there – it fades. And me and my mother wake one
    morning and the furniture's all gone and only these three
    plastic seats and the ticket machine and the radio and then
    his voice from the other side of the wall telling us we needed
    to wait. And I stand by the window and look out at the city –
    and had I noticed back then that there were fewer people
    walking around and more towers quietly being built?
    (*Pause.*) And at what age was I left alone? I turn from the
    window and she's gone. She's with your family and made
    part of something, he says. Can I leave and see my mother
    and be with them? Wait to be called. I'll help you, he says.
    (*Slight pause.*) I wait – and I dream like he tells me to. He
    talks them from me and tells me that outside they're being
    built for me, those dreams.

A pause.

The curtain fell down yesterday. I stretched up and looked
outside. I saw the seagulls flying through the towers and out
towards the sea. No houses or shops or offices – only towers
and nothing else.

A pause.

I could see them in their rooms like me. Hunched over and
holding their tickets like me. (*Slight pause.*) So many
thousands of us. (*Pause.*) And from one tower they're falling
out from their windows.

She covers her eyes.

I make myself watch them. (*Slight pause.*) They're falling like leaves. (*Slight pause.*) They're cleaning their dead bodies off the streets.

A long pause.

YOUNG MAN. He called me and told me to come to this room. When I did he was lying here dead.

A pause.

ISLA. And why did he call you?

YOUNG MAN. I clean the rooms when they're empty. I clean them before the next people enter. (*Slight pause.*) His work with you was done. (*Slight pause.*) It's your time to leave.

The LED screen changes. It stops on number '5824'.

Music and we're thrown into near-darkness.

A previously unseen slim door on the back wall opens slowly and a shaft of light comes through it.

The YOUNG MAN *stands up from the control desk.*

ISLA *turns towards the open door.*

She slowly undresses herself to her underwear and throws her clothes on the pile of clothes in the corner.

She leaves the room and the door closes behind her.

Suddenly the music cuts and a new lighting state.

Scene Two

Silence.

There's a YOUNG WOMAN *in the room.*

The LED screen changes and flicks onto '8461'.

Music.

She dances her final twenty minutes.

At the very end she falls from the window to the outside.

The lights change – the music continues.

Scene Three

A light comes up on the YOUNG MAN *from Scene One.*

Much time has passed and he's sitting (barefoot) in one of the plastic seats.

His face is badly beaten – his body extremely weak from incessant torture.

The music stops.

A light comes up in the control room but there's no one there.

Nothing for several moments.

Then –

The radio switches on and the theme music to the drama is heard.

The radio play begins –

MAUREEN. Good morning, Michael!

MICHAEL. Oh my God I wish it was. The terrible wind out there!

MAUREEN. Don't you like the wind?

MICHAEL. Sure the wind is no friend to man.

MAUREEN. Isn't it?

MICHAEL. For drying clothes and seed propagation – but besides that – the wind is an awful nuisance.

MAUREEN. And how's Martin?

MICHAEL. Martin's just fine.

MAUREEN. Is he?

MICHAEL. He is yeah.

MAUREEN. Look, that's not what I heard. As a friend I think that it's only fair that I raise this worry with you, Michael.

MICHAEL. A worry? Is it a worry, Maureen?

MAUREEN. Well yes it is.

MICHAEL. Or is it just malicious gossip!

MAUREEN. Look – the word is… Martin's acting a little strange…

MICHAEL. Enough of this rubbish! Martin is my son, Maureen! My son! Yes in the past he has been wayward! We all know that! No one will ever forgive him the time he accidently shot those budgies!

The radio suddenly stops.

A pause.

The LED screen makes a noise and the number changes. He doesn't look at it.

A pause.

Breath is heard.

The voice of the female SUPERVISOR –

SUPERVISOR. It's nice when you talk about your childhood.

A slight pause.

And you seem to really enjoy it, I can tell – and they're such fantastic stories anyway…

YOUNG MAN. Haven't you heard them all before?

SUPERVISOR. How could I ever answer that? And even so there's other words you could keep using – unless what you're saying is that you don't want to talk to me – you're being antagonistic on purpose…

YOUNG MAN. I'm sorry.

SUPERVISOR. Oh there's no need to apologise.

A pause.

So do you want me to help you with a story that you can choose?

YOUNG MAN. If you like.

SUPERVISOR. I think it can be easier that way. When I think it's necessary to remind you – I can nudge you a little with words and sound and stuff.

YOUNG MAN. Like before.

SUPERVISOR. Right, exactly, like before. So are you ready?

A slight pause.

YOUNG MAN. Okay.

A pause in which he tries to think of a story to tell.

The SUPERVISOR *begins and immediately everything is heavily scored with detailed sound effects.*

SUPERVISOR. It's your uncle's wedding and you're in this boathouse at the edge of the city.

A pause.

And? (*Slight pause.*) Come on.

A pause.

Sit down on the chair.

The YOUNG MAN *sits.*

Is everything all right?

YOUNG MAN. No.

He cries a little.

SUPERVISOR. No? Why don't you start? – it'll be easier. (*Slight pause.*) Stand up then.

He stands back up.

It's your uncle's wedding and you're in this boathouse at the edge of the city. And?

A slight pause.

YOUNG MAN. And I'm eight years old and my mother's dressed me in this tuxedo – with this… this green cummerbund and matching dicky bow…

SUPERVISOR. And your green patent shoes.

YOUNG MAN. Right and these green patent shoes.

SUPERVISOR. Can you explain it in a funnier way? – it's a little dull.

YOUNG MAN. Sorry.

SUPERVISOR. Oh there's no need to apologise – Let's just start again.

A slight pause.

It's your uncle's wedding and you're in this boathouse at the edge of the city.

YOUNG MAN. And I'm eight years old and my mother's dressed me in this little tuxedo with this green cummerbund and matching dicky bow and these green patent shoes – and I looked a little like a giant sweet wrapper – because back then I was oval in shape – so I looked like I was wrapped around a very big and expensive truffle.

SUPERVISOR. That's much better – didn't it feel much more lively?

YOUNG MAN. I suppose.

SUPERVISOR. And you were almost enjoying it, weren't you? You were almost lost in the moment!

YOUNG MAN. Barely.

SUPERVISOR. Do some actions – make it even more interesting. And you were looking out on the lake – come on!

He begins to badly action his story as lights accompany him.

YOUNG MAN. Well what was the lake – there was no water – but there were three ducks out there and they were – hanging out – barely quacking to each other. Had I been able to put a word on it back then – I would say that they were sort of traumatised – which is impossible to read in a duck's expression – even from up close – but back then – standing in my little tuxedo in that boathouse – looking out on those three ducks moping about in the very middle of that dry lake – they didn't look like they were enjoying themselves – they looked fucking miserable.

SUPERVISOR. And you were feeling hungry.

YOUNG MAN. Yes, I was starving – and it's completely unrelated to seeing the ducks – not that there was any eating in them – though eating them would have saved them from an awfully slow death...

SUPERVISOR. A little morbid, forget about the ducks.

YOUNG MAN. Okay right!

SUPERVISOR. Excellent work though! You're improving, barely.

YOUNG MAN. Thank you.

SUPERVISOR. And energy too!

YOUNG MAN. Yes!

SUPERVISOR. So you turn away from the window looking for food.

YOUNG MAN. Yes, I turn away and there are people dancing – and they're all drunk, naturally – and my dad is barely recognisable to me – because he's – dancing is too tame a word – he's – imagine that he's full of fleas and from every limb he's trying to fling those fleas from out of his body.

SUPERVISOR. Hah!

YOUNG MAN. And there's people looking at him – to avoid being struck by a hand or a foot – and because he's crying. Not ridiculous crying in any way – any big tears were being digested and turned into his sweat and flung off him. He was as dry as that lake outside – while the people around him were being whacked by sweat – but anyone could see his fear. They'd seen it – millions of times – but that doesn't make it any less upsetting.

SUPERVISOR. So you hid.

YOUNG MAN. Right, I hid beneath the buffet table so I could only see legs…!

SUPERVISOR. This is almost getting emotional – do you want to stop?

YOUNG MAN. I don't care.

SUPERVISOR. Because you want to sleep?

YOUNG MAN. Yes, I want to sleep.

SUPERVISOR. So from beneath the table you saw your dad and he stopped dancing.

YOUNG MAN. Yes. And he sat down next to my mother – and didn't say anything – because what could be said. And I couldn't look at them any longer and wanted to busy myself by sedating my hunger – so I reached up and took down a huge bowl of mash potatoes and a serving spoon. And from under the table I can hear my uncle's friends queuing for their trifles and talking about the towers they're working on – and they're bragging about this and that and things they barely know about – and things a child doesn't want to listen to – and so I start at the mash potatoes and pull away from their words…

SUPERVISOR. You eat.

YOUNG MAN. I eat yeah. And I hit this rhythm too – and it's like I'm shovelling mash into that lake and over Dad's dancing and onto those terrible things and images those men were talking about. At some point I take off my cummerbund – and it pings right off me and skids across the dance floor and for no particular reason I even slip off my patent shoes – like as if my feet could ever fill with mash potatoes!

The SUPERVISOR *can be heard laughing. She stops.*

SUPERVISOR. And you slept.

YOUNG MAN. Yeah I slept until the last song – and when I woke it felt so good to have used those two hours for sleep. People filing into their cars and returning to their little homes

– and in the distance they could see the lights from the building sites and the towers – but tonight they wouldn't think about their terrible work. I came out from under the table holding shoes that couldn't go on my swollen feet – and bent right over – heavily pregnant with spuds and looking at the floor. Me, Dad and Mum walking to our car in the car park – each of us unaware of the other – the night horribly still – the future fucking terrifying – the moon ambivalent…

SUPERVISOR. Right, that's enough of that.

The sounds suddenly cut.

The YOUNG MAN *falls to his knees exhausted.*

Do you still want to sleep?

YOUNG MAN. Yes of course I want to sleep!

SUPERVISOR. Stand up then.

He stands.

Where's your ticket?

YOUNG MAN. On the seat.

SUPERVISOR. Where did you take Isla to?

YOUNG MAN. I can't tell you that.

A pause.

A square in the ceiling above him slowly opens. He looks up to it.

SUPERVISOR. Are you sorry now for what you did?

YOUNG MAN. No.

A slight pause.

SUPERVISOR. And why not?

YOUNG MAN. Because I did the right thing.

A slight pause.

SUPERVISOR. You will be broken, you do know that?

A slight pause.

YOUNG MAN. I am broken.

*The Los Saicos version of 'Demolición' begins ominously –
as a projected decimal clock begins to countdown from 2:34
on the back wall.*

SUPERVISOR. Get ready.

*As the vocal blares (2:14) – suddenly a pile of clothes falls
through the hole in the ceiling and on to the ground.*

The overhead security cameras project the YOUNG MAN*'s
live image on the back wall.*

The YOUNG MAN *must try on all the clothes – completing
as many outfits as he can. It is fast chaotic work – there are a
number of difficult garments and hats. He's doing
wonderfully but is undone by a Tudor bodice and its straps.
He frantically tries to regain his previous fast rhythm but is
failing.*

The clock reaches zero – the song ends.

*Exhausted he looks up to the hole in the ceiling – expecting
his prize.*

A single Rich Tea biscuit falls into his hands.

YOUNG MAN (*screams*). Fuck!

*He throws it against the stage-right wall – and collapses on
the ground – him only lit now.*

A taped message is loudly turned on –

SUPERVISOR. And not too far in the past – and what passes as
life – the exhaustion of it – the getting up and stepping out –
the choice of which road to travel – the journey to that point
– to read and write and learn – and stretch and age – before
the open door and the many roads – to grow they call it – to
ferment amongst others – and older brothers and sisters –
only born and building towards what?

Music.

*Hundreds of faces of people of various ages are seen on the
back wall – projected quickly – one second for each image.*

And bottled and pushed out ready for the many roads – and
not too long ago – stepping out into all this choice – Christ!
– and seen from above what terrible clamour – no better
than ants, someone said – and ridicule at first – to think of
all we've made – the beautiful shape of things – the
buildings – and ants, you said?! – such art and poetry – and
before progress was shown up for what it is – and bandied
about that word – in time bashed down and shunned – the
chaos of things – once it all tipped over – not that they could
ever see what we could see – well how could they ever? –
those other ones – doors open and carving up Earth into
eight billion pieces – hungry little grabbing bastards –
they're out now – is it any wonder the word 'ants' – there's
less ridicule and smaller outcry – people quietly praying for
war just to remove – to ease – the natural order not
whispered now – and not too far in the distance – a
forgotten reason – and how many died exactly? – a fraction
– was it only ten? – a blip said the man who first said ants –
and reformed as before – 'cause we can't stop making each
other – ten million remade and fucked into life, he said –
and again hungry little grabbing bastards – where not even
wars can shut down the reckless spirit and terrible clamour
of humans – and not one voice – for quietly it formed –
whispered – less than that – invisible in the breeze it came –
later it would be driven and shaped and bettered – without
words at the very start – an instinct, let's call it – an instinct
to clean up – never said those words but felt in everyone –
it's the 'lower ones' – to keep them stupid and guessing –
and exactly what would? – is it possible even? – not too
long ago – bloody ants! – it's said freely now – and loudly –
in words – and fed into phones – and progress smashed and
shaped into – beyond the tipping point. What if they were
kept? – what if there were less roads – what if there were
only two roads? – those keeping and those being kept – and
at first horror when spoken – when made whole this idea –
when said – but felt in everyone – felt in those ones quietly
praying for wars – from small seeds and hidden away – and
grown in dark corners until it can be held up as an answer
this idea – and whispered at first out into the wider world –
how large can they grow those towers? – how many can

they build? – and felt in everyone – in everyone that matters that is – that whisper grows – out from the darker corners of the world – and taken as the New Way – the New Course – and sold and bought – and board up the windows and keep them busy – and tear up all that was before – ripped and rethought – and no clamour and noise but an order to all things – and seen from above these towers – not a noise – not a squeak – not a word...

Lights up immediately – considerably brighter than before –

You shouldn't be frightened of being killed – we don't ever kill people in the way that you'd imagine.

YOUNG MAN. I know that.

SUPERVISOR. And that's why you're frightened?

YOUNG MAN. Yes.

SUPERVISOR. Excellent joke, you little shit. And where did you take her?

YOUNG MAN. Out of the city.

SUPERVISOR. Where to out of the city?

YOUNG MAN. I won't tell you.

SUPERVISOR. Why didn't you stay with her?

YOUNG MAN. 'Cause you'd find her if she was with me.

SUPERVISOR. To protect her you came back? –

YOUNG MAN. Yes.

SUPERVISOR. – Why would you do all of that?

YOUNG MAN. Because I liked her.

SUPERVISOR. And because of what you saw before you saw her? –

YOUNG MAN. Yes.

SUPERVISOR. – The other woman in that other tower – because of her and what happened...? –

YOUNG MAN. Yes.

SUPERVISOR. – Her dying wouldn't be wasted – Tell me what you saw that morning!

YOUNG MAN. No.

SUPERVISOR. Do you want to sleep? –

YOUNG MAN. Yes!

SUPERVISOR. – Where's your ticket?

YOUNG MAN. On the seat, where it was before!

SUPERVISOR. Are you waiting to be called?!

YOUNG MAN. Of course not!

SUPERVISOR. Then why did you take a ticket?!

YOUNG MAN. Because you told me to fucking take a ticket!!

The YOUNG MAN *screams with frustration.*

A louder sudden surge of sound and light.

He falls to the ground and smashes his fist against the ground – over and over –

Blackout.

Lights immediately up.

SUPERVISOR. Fuck it! Get up!

The YOUNG MAN *slowly gets up.*

So?

A pause.

If you tell me what you saw – I'll let you sleep.

A slight pause.

YOUNG MAN. Do you promise you will?

A slight pause.

SUPERVISOR. Yes. (*Slight pause.*) Mostly.

A pause.

The YOUNG MAN *walks over to the microphone attached to the wall – his hand drips blood.*

A light slowly comes down on him.

A stilled moving image appears on the back wall.

It's a glass door with a sign, 'ARLINGTON', in black lettering written above it.

The YOUNG MAN *looks back at it.*

This is right, isn't it?

YOUNG MAN. Yes.

A pause.

SUPERVISOR. You're woken that morning very early.

The YOUNG MAN *turns away from the image and faces the microphone.*

A pause.

Music.

YOUNG MAN (*his voice amplified*). And there's a message from that man telling me to come to this room and to clean it. That the woman there is to be called later that day and moved to a new tower.

A pause.

SUPERVISOR. And.

A pause.

YOUNG MAN. And I dress and leave my building and walk the road. And I see only a few other people making the journey further into the city – I watch them disappearing into the buildings – going about their work like me.

SUPERVISOR. And.

YOUNG MAN. And in the quietness I hear a noise that I can't understand. I turn onto a new road and stop. (*Slight pause.*) And there's pieces of a man lying on the path and about him others from the building come outside and in moments the path is cleaned. (*Slight pause*.) Old blood has stained the road – the fresh blood is left to dry – the quietness again.

A pause.

SUPERVISOR. And.

A pause.

YOUNG MAN. I turn away from my journey and go into that tower where he'd fallen from.

The image on the back wall begins to move as it enters Arlington Tower and moves up the stairs.

And without a thought my legs walk me up the stairs inside and past the rooms I walk on and up. From inside their rooms they can hear my footsteps – and they're calling to me to let them out.

During the below the lights and images are beginning to falter.

Further on and up – and I can't hear my steps any more and only their voices – the screaming. (*Slight pause*.) Fuck. (*Slight pause*.) And now I want for the very top – for the outside and the sky and the cold air.

Blurred images of the YOUNG WOMAN *we saw dancing before she killed herself – fade up on the back wall*.

I stop at two doors. One to the roof and the other one – a small glass square on the door looking into this last room – to her. (*Slight pause*.) And not screaming like the others. (*Slight pause*.) Promised a dream and her ticket in hand – and walked from one tower to this one – and locked in this new room with its open window. To break her. To break all of them. (*Slight pause*.) I make myself look at her.

A pause.

I push the door out on to the roof and look out on all that I've helped to build and keep. (*Slight pause*.) And to fall fast and feel the air like her – to let that air rip out my insides – and to hit the ground and be done.

A long pause.

I can see a line of green and countryside beneath the dawn.
Far in the distance on the edge of this city – it's hope out
there. Real hope.

*A sudden surge of sound and light – significantly stronger
than before.*

A single light on the YOUNG MAN *as he falls to the ground
and covers his head.*

*A deep pounding guttural noise fills the auditorium as the
images of the* YOUNG WOMAN *dancing begin to distort.*

The room's trying to fix itself but failing.

*Past images are projected erratically – they chew themselves
up – and catch fire.*

*The ceiling tiles are being peeled back – above them a
bigger space.*

After one minute the noise and images implode.

Silence for some moments.

The YOUNG MAN *slowly looks up – and as he does the
light on him opens wider.*

A completely new atmosphere – new light.

He is somewhere else.

ISLA *is standing against the stage-left wall looking over at
him – she's wearing his old shirt, her skirt and runners. The
ceiling above them is sixty per cent open.*

A long pause as they look across at each other.

Then –

ISLA. Do you have a favourite food?

A long pause.

YOUNG MAN. Like a type of food?

A pause.

ISLA. Like any type at all – a food type.

A long pause.

YOUNG MAN. Biscuits – strangely.

ISLA. Right.

YOUNG MAN. And you?

ISLA. The same.

YOUNG MAN. And any particular type?

ISLA. No.

YOUNG MAN. It sort of feels unfair to choose –

ISLA. – each one has their own qualities.

YOUNG MAN. Right.

A long pause.

ISLA. Is it wrong to call biscuits an invention?

A pause.

YOUNG MAN. No I don't think so.

A pause.

ISLA. I think they're probably the greatest invention ever created.

YOUNG MAN. I think you're absolutely right.

A long pause.

ISLA. Do you have a favourite animal you've never seen.

A pause.

YOUNG MAN. Of course.

ISLA. Mine's a dog.

YOUNG MAN. A dog? Any particular type of dog, Isla?

A long pause.

ISLA. How many types are there?

YOUNG MAN. There's a lot.

ISLA. Oh – that makes for a trickier decision…

YOUNG MAN. Why are we doing this?

A slight pause.

ISLA. What do you mean?

YOUNG MAN. Why are we talking about dogs and biscuits?

A slight pause.

ISLA. Because it's something we didn't do when we walked
from the city – we didn't say anything to one another. (*Slight
pause.*) I walked on a little further through the woods that
you brought me to and turned around and you had gone
back. (*Slight pause.*) To save me?

A long pause.

YOUNG MAN. A baby elephant. A favourite animal.

She smiles.

The YOUNG MAN *stands up against the stage-right wall –
and* ISLA *stays against the stage-left wall – looking across
at each other.*

Above them the gentle sound of the wind is heard.

Then quietly – carefully –

ISLA. The steps on the stairs they unfold themselves as we pass
– and down and each room and floor and brick and door –
they press into one another – and memories and sad pasts
lose themselves in the bad dust. And you open the door to
the outside and take my hand.

A pause.

And we're pointed west – and behind our backs the towers
quietly pull towards each other. And concrete and glass return
to clay and sand and the road peels away behind us and it too
turning to dust. And then the wind it takes all they built – and
it's sent upwards and lost out in space in seconds. And we
walk on with our hearts in time – our heads still bowed against
all they made – but in our hands we rewrite pictures of us
alone – all heartache disappearing – and new things start with
us – with you here walking us towards this hope. With love.

A long pause. Then quietly –

YOUNG MAN. Behind us the city lies beneath the ground –
and all bruised it barely hides all it became. We walk away
from it and I take your hand and the countryside folds
around us – a day draws its horizon with promise and
possibility – and we walk further within it – to and through
an open field – the sun on our backs – the horizon lifting
with trees – and this dream taken and made real now. (*Slight
pause.*) 'Cause – being careful underfoot – and little twigs –
and lovely uneven ground – and our fingers passing over
trees. And through pools of sunlight bent through branches –
and sitting down together and warming our faces – and
catching again our childhood this sun – and gently fall the
leaves. We're faced forward and towards – promise. (*Slight
pause.*) Today our spirit will walk a distance. (*Slight pause.*)
The moment will continue. (*Slight pause.*) The day will lead
us. (*Slight pause.*) It will last this feeling.

A pause.

Music.

Standing opposite each other now and she takes his hand.

Then –

YOUNG MAN. Where do you think I am?

A pause.

ISLA. I think you're here with me.

A pause.

YOUNG MAN. But where is that?

A pause.

ISLA. Sitting with me in these woods.

A pause.

YOUNG MAN. Is that true?

ISLA. Yes.

A pause.

YOUNG MAN. When will I be there again, Isla?

A pause.

ISLA. When it's over. (*Slight pause.*) Soon.

They kiss.

ISLA sits on one of the plastic seats and the YOUNG MAN curls up beside her and places his head on her lap.

She talks words we can't hear. As he listens to her he begins to sleep.

Over one minute the lights slowly fade down on them.

Leaves begin to gently fall through the ceiling.

ISLA carefully stands up from the YOUNG MAN – so as not to wake him.

She walks away – stops – and stares up to the window.

The music continues for some moments.

Blackout.

The End.

ROOM 303

This version of *Room 303* premiered at the Festival Gallery, Market Street, Galway, on July 13, 2014, as part of the Galway International Arts Festival.

Featuring the voice of Niall Buggy

Director	Enda Walsh
Design	Paul Fahy
Scenic Artist	Ger Sweeney
Sound Engineers	Joe Birditch and Helen Atkinson

Room 303 was first produced as part of the Sixty-Six Books season at the Bush Theatre, London, on October 13, 2011, also performed by Niall Buggy, and directed by Madani Younis.

Character

MAN

In a cheap, chaotic hotel room – a MAN*'s voice is heard.*

On a matter of principle I would always set out to accomplish that which needs finishing. It's in my nature to finish things. I could tell you all manner of stories from my youth that would prove to you that I have that quality but you know this – of course you do – in the past I've spoken to you about this probably – it doesn't seem wildly important to go into that sort of detail just yet.

There are lots of words for what I am now – but where I am is in this room – this hotel room. At least it seems like it could be a hotel room. All indications suggest that it isn't. It's been a long time cleaned certainly. I can't see the floor. The carpet – if it is carpeted – is thick with – what exactly? I don't like looking at the floor and stay lying in the bed – or very occasionally sitting up in bed and talking as I am now – just to prove that I can sit up in a bed and talk.

I felt a twinge in my back the other day – which proves that I still have a little muscle – unfortunately. It reminds me of the years of walking – of stepping off buses – of arriving in new towns and knocking on doors and speaking then the good word to strangers – and occasionally being invited into their homes and sharing with them hot beverages and of course a saucer of biscuits. Always the confectionery! And I would leave their homes – leave them brimming with a new hope – and other men I would see leaving other houses and stepping back on to buses and travelling the country just like me with our words.

I had working muscles back then – now I'm more of a quilt in substance. Now I'm more of the bed – belong to the bed – my country is this room – my town is this mattress – my home is my head – and ordinarily I would finish a task – as you know I would – on principle I would – I would have to – but is it possible to finish this thought even – to finish this breath – this idea of me? This is the crux – as they say – of the matter.

The other day there was a fly in the room – in my country, let's keep calling it – a fat bluebottle, to give it its correct term – and he barely buzzed – so fat he was. I could see him at the far end of the country over there. He was on my papers. It was almost like he was half-reading those words – and he panted about in an asthmatic sort of way – shuffling from one line to the next – hardly looking for Enlightenment – probably looking for food matter – In here?! Anyway – he stopped his reading and seemed to be looking back at me. He then – miraculously – flew.

He was Malteser in size and an azure blue in colour and as he approached I was repulsed by this beast. How much shit had he licked in his short lifetime this fat fly? He landed where my legs are. He licked around my quilt but all the time with the intention of making his way closer to my face – which he did! And there was something in his fat swagger that suggested that he saw in me an equal. That after perusing my papers he saw in me – a beast of similar ambition to him – of similar worth – of similar purpose to him – the bastard!

A pause.

Surprisingly, it was never my intention to play out my last days being stared at by a fat bluebottle in a shitty hotel room. Dreams of dying were always dreams of friends or strangers I had talked to – people I had given the good word to in return for hot beverages and biscuits. I would be dying on a bed and these people would surround that bed and kind words would float down on me and ease me into my death and towards my God – my Heaven. This is the dream. This is what teases me in moments of lucidity. Ordinarily I am a man who finishes a task – I will not allow another thought to end before finding some rest!

A slight pause.

I will not allow that fly to wither me with his arrogance.

A slight pause.

Amazingly I had enough breath in me to send him toppling over this bed and into the terrible abyss of the floor. The shit! No doubt he's feeding off the remnants down there – feeding off whatever substance there is down there. But the breath does not lie! The breath tells me of my life – that I have a life still! That I must gather something from this room. That through the room's refuse I must find again what truth is! I must!

A pause.

What was it I stepped off those buses with? What was the thing we brought into strangers' houses? What were the good words that came from my mouth? This is the crux – as they say – of the matter. Of me.

A pause.

And it must be a hotel room, surely! On either side of me I can hear voices. Televisual voices with their suggestion of a world continuing – of adventure and geographies and colour. My television ceased transmission months ago. I had it running continually to drown out – difficult to put a word on it – difficult to say what exactly is emoting inside this head and needed drowning out. Anyway the fucker broke down. Some time during *Bargain Hunt* it died – gave up the ghost – kicked the televisual bucket!

And it's not a theory – I have made it a fact! It *is* a hotel room! It must be! A hotel I have often visited – we have often visited. And we would meet in the mornings at breakfast – and over our breakfasts we would again define goodness to one another – and we would write our papers and step on buses and arrive in towns and knock on doors and offer hope and drink their hot beverages. Our good words began, you see, in these hotels. In a hotel room like this one.

The theory is – the theory that must now be a fact – is that these rooms are full of us – full of men like me. It was always men like me – of my colour and type and sound. Men with my words, with my amount of words. That was the way it was – and here we are – in hotel rooms that are now our countries – in homes that are now our heads – unable to breakfast with one another and talk again of what it is we believe in any more! At least the men on either side of me have *Bargain Hunt*! At least they have the clatter of daytime television to stave off what I must now face here alone in the silence, in the darkness with a fat bluebottle for company! My God!

A long pause and only his breath.

And it's something I don't like to do – have not done for some time now – but must.

A slight pause.

Do it!

A pause.

I look down from the bed. Down at what was the floor...

... and pictures there – of a house I was taken home to and sisters and brothers in their best clothes and a dog who once shared this house and a garden crisp in black and white but a yellow car – and my father with sleeves and trousers rolled up, a cigarette in his mouth not yet lit and me in his arms.

And scenes in a new house with another garden and the gate that led to the open road and the feeling still of the freshly cut grass tickling the backs of my legs as I'm sat under an inflatable paddling pool with Sinead such-and-such kissing me or rather plunging her tongue into my mouth and telling me it was called 'kissing'.

And faster the images come and fill the floor with smells of youth and half-dreamt stories of Dollymount Strand and the sea in front and breaking hearts and pulverising livers and the smell of sex in every breath and an idea of the world and my involvement in that world and burning friendships and terrible indifference and insatiable lusts and sweet vodka and everyday boredom.

And amongst the remnants a clearer more isolated me – a broken self-hating me – an insignificant vocally retarded young man who continues to show half-notions of himself and proclaims half-truths of himself and sells them as gospel to strangers who cram together and nod barely.

And through the clatter of my younger years and falling deeper now into the floor and into the quick burn of happiness of my later years – deluded in its ridiculous importance but briefly it seems rescued – rescued by His words.

And joined to others and breakfasts and bus journeys and spreading those words like new air until all there is is God's truth and my body ageing.

A pause.

That truth now forgotten. Gone. Completely.

A pause.

And the remnants clear a little further – fall away – evaporate around one another – the carpet disintegrating with nothing to hold it now – memories disappearing as a larger breath takes them.

A pause.

I look down from this bed into the big space beneath me…

…and there…

…I can see a man lying in his bed… lying beneath his quilt… And he's staring back up at me.

And he too is talking with frightened eyes. Holding on for a few seconds more of life – like I too hold on for life. And his words I can't hear.

A slight pause.

I don't know what it is he's saying. No one knows.

A slight pause.

Not even he.

The End.

A GIRL'S BEDROOM

The world premiere of *A Girl's Bedroom* took place at the Bank of Ireland Theatre, National University of Ireland, Galway, on July 13, 2015, as part of the Galway International Festival.

Featuring the voice of Charlie Murphy

Director	Enda Walsh
Design	Paul Fahy
Scenic Artist	Ger Sweeney
Sound Engineers	Nick Sykes and Helen Atkinson

Character

YOUNG WOMAN

Lights are already up as we enter a six-year-old girl's bedroom.

When the door is closed – and after a few moments – we hear a YOUNG WOMAN*'s voice.*

At bedtime – when I was six – and before I left – I used to ask my dad to retell stories from his childhood. At the beginning – let's say the first three times he would tell me whatever it was he was telling – there was some enjoyment, maybe – he seemed to be enjoying the telling. He wasn't hating it like he was when I asked him the twentieth time or whatever. He used stand in my bedroom like he was made of clay – hunched over – stripping all colour from his words and wanting for his television downstairs – claiming he couldn't remember every 'bloody detail', that he was 'so tired', that 'you've heard the story dozens of times before – so what's the point anyway!?'

I remember the dull sound of the living-room door closing and the television spitting on and my parents moderately drinking wine and eating the hidden chocolate and murmuring whatever it was adults murmur.

I'd start to talk to my room – inventing stories for bears and dolls — the darkness terrifying outside – the room filling with stories of unrequited love, obviously – with neglect, definitely and deceit – a vengeful Barbie travelling beneath my bed to punish a Sylvanian bunny and so on – And all of this played to the noise of the television under my carpet – two worlds bound together by blood and walls.

Theirs and mine.

I'd stop my playing – sit on my bed – and try to imagine them as me – for maybe they were once as I am – or was – back then when I was six.

How is it that they have grown into this half-life?

And I could feel the pull of the downstairs – like the little world I had built in my bedroom would soon crack to the terrible beigeness of the rest of their house. With this anxiety I puked big on the little rug. In that state – my brain dressed me for the darkness outside. In those clothes – I stood up in the middle of my room – my six-year-old self turning slowly – scanning the room blankly – looking over toys like some queen – like an empress beginning a larger unknowable journey – being pulled from this pink place with no stain on me – but for a mouth coated in puke.

A pause.

I walked past the living-room door with all that world my parents had created inside – the two of them barely existing in there to me.

I moved to the outside then.

Out into the darkness.

The room very slowly fades into darkness during the below.

With the door left open – my legs carry me – and at first I look to the ground – not wanting to see the familiar streets – and I pass through what we called 'The Green' – a tiny square of pockmarked muck shredded by football boots – and portions of dogshit in which my pink runners then skid. To the seafront and buckled tarmac and only then raising my head – the wind taking my chin – and turning my eyes upwards to a sky dangerously dark. Only an hour since I left my bedroom and each step walks in a less familiar place. The seafront disappearing for a while into a road and other houses then.

Through windows the night is marked out – people slouch by televisions – others stand and scratch themselves – others enter bedrooms – see to curtains – extinguish lights – families sleep – rooms darken – cars less frequent now – the outskirts of the city fades to my walking and countryside – and just a heartbeat.

Around me still the smell of my room – and with it the lure of my old things – but other thoughts scratch in the darkness – where I'm sitting in the back of our car and we're singing to a song on the radio – the three of us out of time – where we're walking in the woods – each taking a separate path – and sitting then silently in restaurants like we're strangers – three people kept by association.

The walk continues through the night – the darkness evaporates those thoughts – and the walk becoming easier and lighter in the dawn – in the day. The memory of them – of their faces – of the bedroom – for now – it dulls.

A pause.

Just me and the walking.

A pause.

The countryside slopes back down to the coast – and with it I walk the line between the land and sea – the water marking out days with tides. Over sharp rocks – and following the coast folding back in on itself – the prize of a beach opens up – the steeliness of sea on sand – I hum a tune to remind me of my voice. I can see figures on a cliff – or far in the distance someone in the sea – silent dots on every other horizon losing themselves in the bigger picture – while I pierce that picture with some purpose and this walking.

The weather warming and moving over a coastline spotted with families having shitty picnics in the sand – or perched in the back of their cars like budgies eating Pringles. They turn as I pass – my clothes shredded by the walk – my once-pink runners bleached and aged in rock pools. Food is scavenged in bins, stolen from cars, from witless families gawping at this runaway girl.

Time buckles quickly then and lit by a fire – the sea and wind shouts above what sounds like my voice trying to talk stories for itself but failing.

And later and blown inland and passing through small towns – the walk continues without direction – its purpose unknown to me. Always foot after foot where weeks merge into months – and collected snatches of pictures pass through hedgerows – where down a road I run and chased by a dog – and cliff-sitting and eating chips – and curled up in the long grass caught between asleep and awake – and terrified of the night-time sky always – yet powered by this freedom in daytime.

Somewhere – sometime – I stop walking.

A pause. The room is now completely dark but for a small fluorescent solar-system mobile hanging from the ceiling.

For days I think only of my bedroom.

And is it as it was?

A pause.

The details already forgotten.

A pause.

Think.

A pause.

A wooden bed, probably – and scuffed by my nails these stickers of something – and a carpet of what colour? – and a small pink rug, I think – and wallpaper – and random soft toys that are gathered in little crowd scenes awaiting a presentation of one of my stories – and precious pictures Blu-Tacked for some forgotten reason – and boxes of hairbands and clips and lost bracelets – knotted and broken.

A pause.

And through that pink haze – I can see overhead, small planets hanging from a ceiling – a sky I always loved – a sky that never frightened me.

Not once.

A pause.

I try to pull together all the indifference, all this imagined coldness between them and me – I try to raise the volume of their television in my mind and see again loudly their disdain for that daughter in the bedroom upstairs.

I try – but see nothing.

No coldness. No indifference.

A pause.

The thought then –

A pause.

– there was no reason to run.

A pause.

My walking turns in on itself – it scratches the edges inside and has me turning back and longing for that room.

For them and me. For my home.

A pause.

But where is it?

A pause.

Not now six and I'm still lost in a world that drives me on with a purpose that's unknown. Always foot after foot – where time disappears into landscapes.

Where that bedroom sits behind my eyes.

A pause.

Always.

The lights come back on in the room.

The End.

KITCHEN

The world premiere of *Kitchen* took place at The Shed, Galway Harbour, Galway, on July 11, 2016, as part of the Galway International Arts Festival.

Featuring the voice of Eileen Walsh

Director	Enda Walsh
Design	Paul Fahy
Scenic Artist	Ger Sweeney
Sound Design	Helen Atkinson

Character

WOMAN

A narrow galley kitchen – two metres wide and six metres in length.

The sideboard and overhanging cabinets are white Formica – the floor an uneventful lino – the walls painted with a mint-green paint.

Everything on the surface is impossibly clean. Spotless.

When the cabinets are opened (as the audience will) – plates and cups can be seen. They've all been smashed into small pieces.

When the washing machine is opened – it is filled with shredded clothes.

When the oven is opened – it is filled with burnt toast.

The sink is in front of a window with a net curtain over it.

There is a constant grey light through this window. The curtain can't be peeled back to look outside.

Somewhere there's a cork pinboard – one metre in length. Pinned to it are hundreds of images of birds – badly cut out from various newspapers and magazines. It is a significant blast of colour in an otherwise bland kitchen space.

There's no light overhead – but the ceiling is white perspex, from which light shines. As the audio continues the brightness intensifies in the kitchen until the final minute – which is unbearably bright.

When the kitchen door is closed behind the audience – the voice of a WOMAN *can be heard.*

1.

He says that I do this often – that often there's nothing there – that through my eyes I make it something that it isn't. Why do you do that? Why do you look at something and make it mean another thing? Sometimes something doesn't have a story. Sometimes a chair is only a chair! I've never stopped being anxious. My first human contact was with forceps. Just wanting an embrace – and to be pinched and plucked out. To be a nail stuck into my mother and feel about me that extraction – which accounts – which may account – which must account for the way in which I see a chair not as a chair – but something much darker than a chair. Why do you see the bad in everything? Because of the forceps, I want to say! The bloody forceps! Have you any idea how sore it is to be dragged out of your sleep by a wrench? To be pulled from your rest like you were a rotten tooth! I want to say these things – I never say these things – I can't say them. You darken a room. Some women lighten a room – can alter the temperature of a room. They can walk into a space and by small degrees the light brightens – or perhaps the weather of that room warms a little. And people are puzzled – and they imagine that someone's fiddling with the light switch or the thermostat – they're taking off their jacket or averting their eyes from the brighter light – until someone says – and they probably say it in a knowing voice – they say to the others – 'A woman has walked into this room! The room is not the same. The room is a better place because this woman has entered it. Soon she'll be gone and it'll be back to what it was – but for now – while she is present – this room has been changed for the better!' Some women are like that. But not you. You're like a cloud – dark obviously and full of rain – without the expression of rain. You're like a cancer-cloud. Which wasn't a very surprising thing to say – though it surprised him and had him circling around various medical and meteorological metaphors – in which he asked me – What was squeezed out of your ear by those forceps? Was it gladness? Was jauntiness pinched out of your head? At your birth – did merriment fall on to the floor – was it trodden underfoot and mopped up as they wheeled mother 'n' child outside to meet dozy Daddy? What

have you done with the plates in the cabinets, the clothes in the
machine, the smell of burnt toast, woman!? Why do you stand
there by the sink with your back to me? Why don't you say…

A sudden loud muffled thud noise – one second long…

Immediately – the next day.

2.

Why are you still standing there? Why are you standing by the
sink in that way still? Have you moved? Why haven't you
moved since yesterday when I made that joke about you
resembling a cancerous cloud? I didn't answer for fear I'd break
up and words would tumble out and never stop. Like a pot
being filled with water I stood there – and what words would
wet my slippers – and higher to ankle deep – words about birth
– for I am nothing but chronological! And though silent of
course – I'm moving upwards through my childhood – stories
related by my dark-cloud-existence. A happy-birthday scene
and me itching in a mohair cardigan – staring at the flames of
my tenth year – terrified to my stomach of the next ten years.
Knee-deep and words lap above the lino – and further I talk into
my teenage years – of boys poking and prodding me like I'm a
dead sea lion. Lost evenings barking by the seafront and
looking for real love. Even now the taste of salt makes me want
to puke. Is this seasoned? Why don't you ever season the food?
Why are you still standing there? Why haven't you moved?
Words flap over the countertop with unspoken stories of
heartache – to be kicked in the heart – to feel that ache from boy
to boy to younger man and then… Can feel him behind me –
he's looking for the salt to season that dinner he made – I stand
still and lose myself further – and I imagine these silent words
at chest height as I skip through stories of our early marriage –
darkening stories of him and us! In this way the kitchen fills
with my past – and over my mouth and nose it rises – till
standing still and underneath my past – and breathless – though
not showing it – and drowning – but not telling him that I am
standing here drowning in our unremarkable past! (*Screams*.)
Why is she standing there? What's she looking at out the
window? Not directed at me but at him – the man she calls her

brother – my husband. I listen to brother 'n' sister addressing
one another but never me. And must I look like a statue? What
if a bird entered and landed on my head? Would I flinch? And
what sort of a bird would I wish for? A myna bird, naturally.
Always a myna. She didn't season your food!? Standing there
since yesterday?! Why hasn't she spoken? Why has she done
that to the plates – to the clothes?! This was never a happy
kitchen – but a wife standing by her sink – unspeaking,
unmoving – it's disgusting! I should have married Sheila when I
had the chance. I was taken in by her dispassion – I imagined
promise underneath her indifference – but she's been nothing
but a dark cloud in my life – a woman who can't see a chair for
a chair! Not only had Sheila a terrific body – she had a sunny
disposition and knew when food needed to be salted! From the
living room she's telling him all about her holiday by the sea in
Spain. I can feel his jealousy drip into the carpet and into the
floorboards. I imagine his head is being squeezed by the picture
of me standing by the sink inside here still. Standing still. I stare
ahead. My fingers grip around the edge of the sink and wh…

A sudden loud muffled thud noise – one second long…

Immediately – the next week.

3.

Gravity's pushing you down – whatever you're trying to prove
by standing there you've failed – 'cause it's no longer you but
someone else standing there – an imposter – a different shape
drawn towards the lino daily – an even worse you. You always
had that sort of a constitution – the sort that would melt like a
dessert. You're melting right now – I can hear your spine
conjoining! Do you close your eyes longer than a blink to wet
your eyes? I crept down in the middle of the night – I pictured
you fast asleep on the couch – but stood still as you are now and
staring at what? Night? At night-time?! He's never spoken as
much as he's speaking now. Given the space and he can't stop
talking the idiot. Is it a week? He says it's a week my standing
still. What started out as something to do – became a thing –
became my whole being. But to what end I ask? Unknown till
this moment – and to speak it out would make it too real – and

having not spoken for a week I'll let the word choose itself
before it's spoken from my mouth and into the kitchen and into
him. Speaking it out will make a definite – speaking it out will
add to his torment – and it is a torment. I can hear him behind at
the table sucking on his cornflakes – his one expression of
happiness is now shaded with misery. Unable to control life he
hangs on the end of his spoon – (*Makes a sucking noise.*)
looking for escape from this! There'll be no escape from here –
here in my kitchen! A room you backed me into – a room to
deny me birds and flight and sky – to tease me with a view
outside a window – to build a wall and block that view! There is
nothing but the end! Inside my head the word forms – letters
gather towards one another – it brightens about me till my
shrunken body fills with this great word – of how I will snap –
of what I am doing and leading to. My fingers grip around the
edge of the sink – my back to him and ears waiting for a pause
in his cornflake-sucking – I hear a little silence – and from my
mouth it proclaims my direction. Disappear, I say out loud.
Disappear! To vanish my purpose, to go, to will annihilation, to
become nothing…

A sudden loud muffled thud noise – one second long…

Immediately – the next month.

4.

He said it that many times it sounded like he couldn't ever leave
– but leave he did. The disappearing is his – the bastard! A spare
room waits silently in my sister's house – you were always
nothing to me – this standing still's a vision of what you always
were and are. You deserve this kitchen! The door closing is the
last sound you'll ever hear! Surprisingly on closing the door the
sounds only begin. Standing still I stare ahead – my fingers grip
around the edge of the sink – ears trying to differentiate this big
sound. In volume the sound grows…

A sudden loud muffled thud noise – one second long…

Immediately – an hour later.

5.

– how many things not said – and friends unmet – and talks not taken – and loves avoided – and children not born – and dreams not made – and paths not walked – and views unseen – and days unspent – and embraces not given or felt – and songs not learnt – and lies undone…

A sudden loud muffled thud noise – one second long…

Immediately – an hour later.

6.

The big sound is me talking big and loud – to clean myself out of me – to disappear maybe – to be nothing – is it possible?! Or maybe to be a speck – to have no consciousness of what was – and to dream a little – but to live wholly, how? How? To fly out over that wall on the other side of the window – in the place we called the garden – to be over that wall and live as a speck – and to undo all that was – the terrible unescapable kitchen! How many things not said – and friends unmet – and talks not taken – and loves avoided – and views unseen – and days unspent – and embraces not given.

A sudden loud muffled thud noise – one second long…

Immediately – an hour later.

7.

To live out there on the breeze – beyond living and seeing only – but to see and empty myself of him and the kitchen. To will death or live like a speck on the breeze?! Beyond sense and madness only – oh Christ! (*Slight pause*.) Christ! (*Slight pause*.) When I was a little girl I dreamt of falling in love with someone good and living in a comfortable house with a bright kitchen.

A sudden loud muffled thud noise – a half-second long –

When I was a little girl falling I dreamt of in love living in with someone good and a comfortable house with a kitchen bright.

A sudden loud muffled thud noise – a half-second long –

When I was in love a little girl I falling house of living in with someone good and dreamt a comfortable with a kitchen bright.

A sudden loud muffled thud noise – a half-second long –

Falling with a kitchen bright when I was a little girl in love with someone good and dreamt a comfortable house of living I in.

A sudden loud muffled thud noise – a half-second long –

Little girl with someone good.

A sudden loud muffled thud noise – a quarter-second long –

Living in a comfortable love.

A sudden loud muffled thud noise – a quarter-second long –

Falling in a bright house.

A sudden loud muffled thud noise – a quarter-second long –

I dreamt of when I was.

A pause.

With a kitchen.

A sudden loud muffled thud noise – a second long –

A pause.

A sudden loud muffled thud noise – a second long –

A pause.

A sudden loud muffled thud noise – a second long.

Lights out – and then lights immediately up.

The End.

Enda Walsh is a multi-award-winning Irish playwright. His work has been translated into over twenty languages and has been performed internationally since 1998.

His recent plays include *Arlington*, produced by Landmark Productions and Galway International Arts Festival; *Lazarus* with David Bowie at New York Theater Workshop and the King's Cross Theatre, London; *A Girl's Bedroom*, shown at the Galway International Arts Festival; a 'mischievous adaptation' of Roald Dahl's *The Twits* at the Royal Court, London; the opera *The Last Hotel* for Landmark Productions and Wide Open Opera (Edinburgh International Festival, Dublin Theatre Festival, Royal Opera House, London, St Ann's Warehouse, New York); *Ballyturk*, produced by Landmark Productions and Galway International Arts Festival (Galway, Dublin, Cork and the National Theatre, London); *Room 303*, shown at the Galway International Arts Festival; *Misterman*, produced by Landmark Productions and Galway International Arts Festival in Ireland, London and New York; and several plays for Druid Theatre Company, including *Penelope*, which has been presented in Ireland, America and London; *The New Electric Ballroom*, which played Ireland, Australia, Edinburgh, London, New York and LA; and *The Walworth Farce*, which played Ireland, Edinburgh, London and New York, as well as an American and Australian tour.

He won a Tony Award for writing the book for the musical *Once*, which played for three years on Broadway and two years in the West End, and returned to the Olympia Theatre in Dublin.

His other plays include *Delirium* (Theatre O/Barbican), which played Dublin and a British tour; *Chatroom*, which played at the National Theatre and on tour in Britain and Asia; and *The Small Things* (Paines Plough), which played London and at Galway International Arts Festival. His early plays include *Bedbound* (Dublin Theatre Festival) and *Disco Pigs* (Corcadorca).

His film work includes *Disco Pigs* (Temple Films/Renaissance) and *Hunger* (Blast/Film4).